HOW IS SOUND MADE?

by Emily Raij

PEBBLE
a capstone imprint

T0050821

Published by Pebble, an imprint of Capstone.
1710 Roe Crest Drive, North Mankato, Minnesota 56003
capstonepub.com

Library of Congress Cataloging-in-Publication Data
Names: Raij, Emily, author.
Title: How is sound made? / Emily Raij.
Description: North Mankato, Minnesota : Pebble, [2022] | Series: Science inquiry | Includes bibliographical references and index. | Audience: Ages 5-8 | Audience: Grades K-1 | Summary: "Sounds can be loud. Sounds can be soft. We use our ears to hear all kinds of sounds. But how is sound made? Let's investigate to find out about sound!"— Provided by publisher.
Identifiers: LCCN 2021029914 (print) | LCCN 2021029915 (ebook) | ISBN 9781663970619 (hardcover) | ISBN 9781666324990 (paperback) | ISBN 9781666325003 (ebook) | ISBN 9781666325027 (kindle edition)
Subjects: LCSH: Sound—Juvenile literature. | Sound—Experiments—Juvenile literature.
Classification: LCC QC225.5 .R34 2022 (print) | LCC QC225.5 (ebook) | DDC 534—dc23
LC record available at https://lccn.loc.gov/2021029914
LC ebook record available at https://lccn.loc.gov/2021029915

Image Credits
Capstone Studio: Karon Dubke, 1, 6, 9, 10, 13, 14, 20; Shutterstock: Andrey_Popov, 23, antoniodiaz, 29, Axel_Kock, 17, balabolka, Cover (Design Elements), COULANGES, 27, DenisProduction.com, Cover, gritsalak karalak, 28, hansen.matthew.d, 22, ikiverova, 5, Kues, 19, Pheelings media, 25, roycine, 21, Stokkete, 18

Editorial Credits
Editor: Erika L. Shores; Designer: Dina Her; Media Researcher: Jo Miller; Production Specialist: Tori Abraham

TABLE OF CONTENTS

Words in **bold** are in the glossary.

A SOUND INVESTIGATION

It's a great day for the beach! You lie in the warm sand and close your eyes. The ocean waves splash. Wind blows through the trees. These soft sounds could put you to sleep.

Suddenly, you hear a fire truck. The siren gets louder as the truck zooms past. Seagulls squawk. They want your picnic lunch. You're wide awake now!

Quiet sounds. Loud sounds. Some make you feel relaxed. Other sounds are too much! Why are sounds so different? And how do we hear them all?

Let's do a hearing investigation. This will be music to your ears!

You're going to make a musical instrument with glass bottles. Each bottle is filled with a different amount of water. The bottles are lined up in a row. You blow across the top of each one to make sound. It's a bottle band!

You need five of the same glass bottles, water, and five stickers numbered 1 to 5. You can stir a drop of food coloring into the water. It makes it easier to see when you fill the bottles.

Place the bottles flat on a table. Fill one bottle with water. Leave another one empty. Now pour different amounts of water in the other three bottles. One can be half full. Another can be less than half full. The last can be more than half full.

Place sticker 1 on the empty bottle. Put sticker 2 on the full bottle. Stickers 3, 4, and 5 go on the other three bottles.

Now you're ready to blow! How do you think each bottle will sound? Blow across the top of each bottle. Do not put your lips right on them. Can you feel the air blowing over the top? What do you hear?

Does each bottle make the same sound? Now, try changing the sound by blowing harder or softer.

Rearrange the order of the bottles. Blow across the bottles. Does what you hear sound different when the bottles are in a different order?

WHAT IS SOUND?

When you blow across the bottles, air moves inside them. That causes **vibrations**. This moving air is what we hear as sounds.

It takes more time for air to move through the bottles with less water. There is more space for the air to move. These slower vibrations make lower sounds.

Vibrations move fast through the bottles with more water and less air. They make higher sounds. Blowing harder also makes higher sounds. The air moves faster.

HOW DO WE HEAR SOUND?

Remember the ocean waves at the beach? Sound travels in waves too. Waves move through the air to your ear. We cannot see sound waves. But we can hear them. And sometimes we can feel vibrations.

Sound waves are made of **energy**. Sound waves lose energy as they travel. That is why sounds are louder when you are closer to them. The waves have more energy. Sounds are quieter if you are farther away. The waves have less energy.

The waves go inside your ear canal. Then they hit your eardrum. Your eardrum is a small flap of skin at the end of your ear canal. It vibrates from sound waves.

The eardrum sends a message to your brain that you heard a sound. Your brain tells you what the sound is. We have two ears so that we can hear sounds all around us. Our ears also help tell us where sounds are coming from.

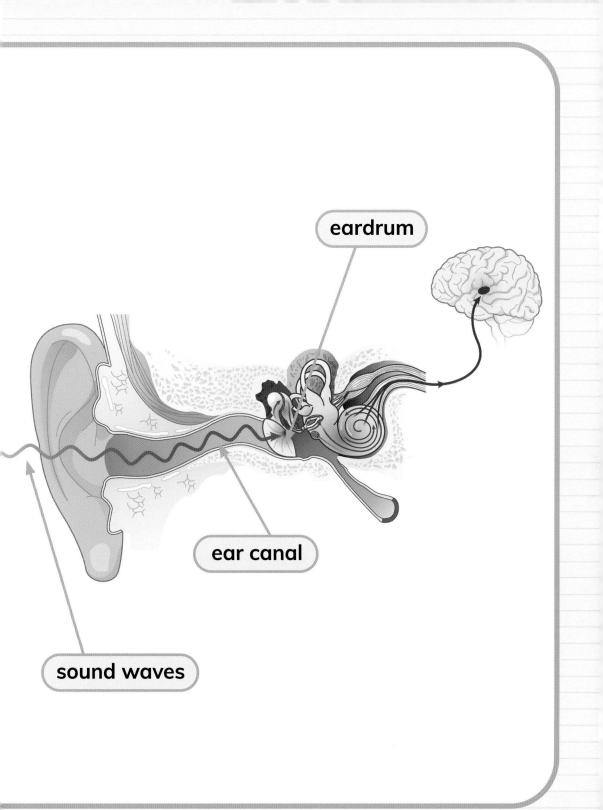

eardrum

ear canal

sound waves

HOW ARE DIFFERENT SOUNDS MADE?

Volume is how loud a sound is. **Amplitude** is how tall a sound wave is. Quiet sounds have less energy and short sound waves. They have a low volume and small amplitude. A whisper or a cat purring are quiet sounds.

Loud sounds have more energy and tall sound waves. They have a large amplitude. Airplanes and fire alarms make loud sounds. Their waves push harder on our eardrums.

Test it out. Clap softly. Now clap harder. It's louder! Its sound waves have more energy.

HOW IS SOUND MEASURED?

We can measure sound waves. **Frequency** is the number of waves moving per second. Sound waves are measured in hertz. Low-frequency sounds are 500 hertz or fewer. High-frequency sounds are 2,000 hertz or more.

Pitch is how low or high a sound is. High sounds move in waves close together. A whistle has a high pitch and a high frequency. Low sounds move in waves farther apart. Thunder has a low pitch and a low frequency.

Some sounds are too low or high for people to hear or make. But not for animals! African elephants make a low sound people can't hear. Other elephants can hear it miles away!

Sometimes parts of the ears don't work. Then people can't hear well or at all. That is called hearing loss or **deafness**. A hearing aid can help people hear. It makes sounds louder or clearer. People can also use sign language. They use hand **signals** instead of spoken words.

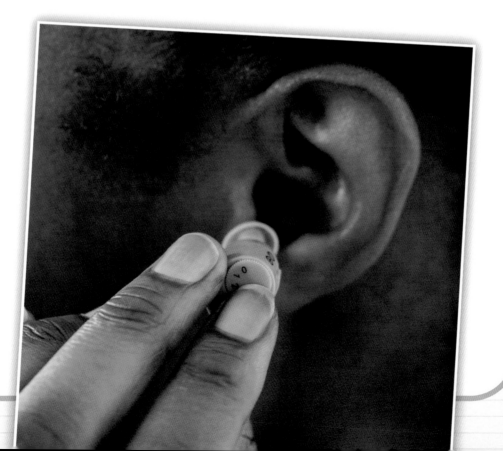

Sometimes sound waves hit something and bounce back. We hear an **echo**. Sounds bounce best off smooth, hard surfaces. Soft surfaces **absorb** sound waves. They can't bounce. All sounds run out of energy. The waves stop bouncing off objects. That is why we don't keep hearing a sound forever.

Sound can travel through air, water, and objects. It travels fastest through solid objects and slowest through gas. Sound waves travel 1,125 feet (343 meters) per second in air.

There is a place where sound waves can't travel. Space! Space has no air for the waves to travel through. That means no sounds can be heard.

HOW DO WE USE SOUND?

Sounds send messages. An alarm warns us of danger or wakes us up.

Animals make different sounds. Cats purr to show happiness. Rattlesnakes shake their tails to show they are ready to bite. Animals use sound to warn and attract mates. They show feelings too. So do people! Babies cry to show they are hungry or scared.

Bats, dolphins, and whales use **echolocation**. They make sounds and listen for echoes. Then they can tell how far away something is. This helps them find food and their way around in the dark.

Ships use **sonar**. That is echolocation under water. Ships send out sound waves. The waves bounce off objects. Ships pick up the echoes. They can tell what objects are in the water and how deep they are.

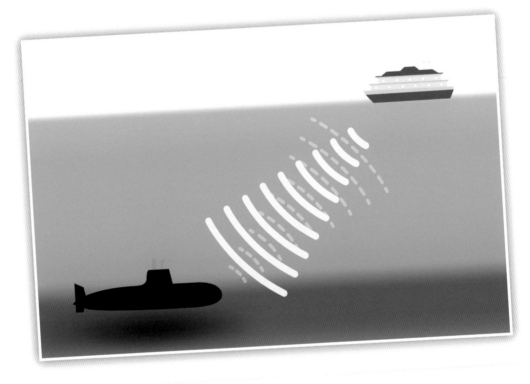

We can change sounds. Microphones turn vibrations into electric signals. They are sent to speakers. Speakers change the signals back to sounds. They also make sounds louder.

Sound helps us communicate and hear the world around us.

GLOSSARY

absorb (ab-ZORB)—to take something in

amplitude (am-PLUH-tood)—the distance from the midpoint of a wave to its crest; a measure of wave strength

deafness (DEF-ness)—the inability to hear

echo (EK-oh)—the sound that returns after a traveling sound hits an object

echolocation (eh-koh-loh-KAY-shuhn)—the process of using sounds and echoes to locate objects; bats, whales, and dolphins use echolocation to find food

energy (E-nuhr-jee)—the ability to do work, such as moving things or giving heat or light

frequency (FREE-kwuhn-see)—the number of sound waves that pass a location in a certain amount of time

signal (SIG-nuhl)—a message between our brains and our senses; hand signals are signs made with your hands to stand for letters, words, or numbers

sonar (SOH-nar)—a device that uses sound waves to find underwater objects

vibration (vye-BRAY-shuhn)—a fast movement back and forth

volume (VOL-yuhm)—the measure of how loud something is

READ MORE

Bernhardt, Carolyn. *Sound*. Minneapolis: Bellwether Media, 2018.

James, Emily. *The Simple Science of Sound*. North Mankato, MN: Capstone, 2018.

Lundgren, Julie K. *Sound: Hear All About It!* New York: Crabtree Publishing, 2022.

INTERNET SITES

How the Human Ear Works
sciencekids.co.nz/videos/humanbody/ear.html

Sound
dkfindout.com/us/science/sound

The Science of Sound for Kids
sciencekids.co.nz/sound.html

INDEX

ABOUT THE AUTHOR

 Emily Raij has written more than 40 books for children and edited dozens of professional resources for K-12 teachers. She lives in Florida with her husband, daughter, son, and dog.